Phonetic Storybook 3

Short ĭ Words

Raceway Step 10

MODERN CURRICULUM PRESS
Pearson Learning Group

Contents

Jim Is Six

By Sue Dickson
Illustrated by Bari Weissman

Vocabulary Words

1. big
2. bit
3. did
4. him
5. hit
6. it
7. Jim
8. miss
9. mitt
10. Ripp
11. Sis

12. six
13. will
14. yip
15. as (az)
16. his (hiz)
17. is (iz)

Story Words

18. can't
19. tell
20. well
21. yet

Jim is six.

Jim is six and big.

Sis can tell Jim is big.

Yes, Dad can tell Jim
is big.
Jim will get as big as
his dad.

Jim can't bat yet.
Dad will help Jim bat.

Dad will help Jim a bit.
Dad will help him
bat well.

Dad can bat well.
Dad can hit!
Jim has a mitt.
Jim can get it.

Jim can miss.
Jim is sad.

Jim can hit.
Dad did help him.
Jim can hit well.
"Yip, yip," went Ripp!

Jim is glad.

The End

Liz and Jill

By Jean Elsie Cox

Illustrated by Rosario Valderrama

Vocabulary Words

1. Bill
2. dip
3. give
4. grins
5. if
6. in
7. Jill
8. lift
9. Liz
10. quick
11. rim
12. slip
13. spin
14. Tim
15. tip
16. tips
17. win
18. wins

Story Words

19. clap

Liz has it.
Liz is fast.
Can Liz get it in?

Liz did miss it.

Jill is quick.
Jill has it.
Jill will slip past Liz.

Jill can lift it.
Can Jill get it in?
Can Jill get it past the
rim?

Jill did miss it.
It hit the rim.

Liz is quick.

Liz gets it.

Liz will dip a bit.

Liz will slip past Jill.

Can Liz get it in?
If Liz can get it past
the rim, Liz can win.

Liz can dip past Jill.

Liz can give it a spin.

It tips the rim.
Can Liz get it in?
Liz can get it in.

Yes! In it went!

Liz is glad.

Liz wins.

Bill and Tim clap.

Liz grins.

The End